*'It is the emotional ally
of intelligence and desire
to mould, to illustrate,
and to make personal
contributions to the age-long
yearnings for humanity
to enliven and decorate
the fringe of laborious life
with a border of beauty.'*

A.L.

Arthur Lismer's Pen and Pencil

A Border
of Beauty

by Marjorie Lismer Bridges

Red Rock   Toronto

A Border of Beauty

Arthur Lismer's pen and pencil

Designed by Tom Sankey

Canadian Cataloguing in Publication Data

Lismer, Arthur, 1885-1969.
  A border of beauty

ISBN 0-920178-04-9

1. Lismer, Arthur, 1885-1969. I. Bridges,
Marjorie Lismer. II. Title.

ND249.L5A22   759.11   C77-001338-4

Red Rock Publishing Co. Limited
474 Avenue Road, Suite 20
Toronto, Canada M4V 2J3

first printing 1977

for Esther
dear wife and mother

A Border
of Beauty

A New Angle on Canadian Art, 1932

Table of Contents

Introduction

"Art is a way of life. It is experience lived, shared, and enjoyed. It is in the painting and the poem. It is in the rhythm and order of nature. It is in the child's drawing as well as in the great periods of art. But it seeks expression. It cannot be a dead spot in the nature of the individual to be revived by historical or civilization memories — or by the erudition of the aesthete. It cannot thrive on words and precepts — only by active expression and self-criticism, by the activities of wise guides and teachers...."

Such was Arthur Lismer's perceptive and enthusiastic view of the world. To my father, an artist was more than an individual who painted and composed. Everyone who looked at life with curiosity and wonder, deeply stirred by his environment, was entitled to the name. Lismer, himself, was an artist in the widest sense of the term. New wonders were constantly opening up before him. His need to communicate these experiences made him both a fine painter and a great teacher.

I do not wish to present an analysis of his paintings nor an evaluation of his teaching. Both are bound up in his life as an artist. He encouraged thousands of young people to see life as he did, with curiosity about themselves and their environment. He insisted that the creative person might draw enrichment from the past, but must always look toward the future.

Lismer, like most men with a message, often talked about writing a book. He wrote extensively for reports, articles, and lectures, but he never found time to get a book ready for publication. He left summaries of several, with chapters roughly outlined. It was a great pity that these were never completed.

The material for this book is from unpublished manuscripts, lecture notes, and his letters. The illustrations are all by Lismer. He left countless small drawings on scraps of paper and backs of menu cards, as well as a large number of sketch books. Manuscripts and drawings together make an accurate commentary on a vivid career. Therefore, this is Lismer's book.

The drawings chosen show the variety of styles and subject matter that came from my father's hand. The trees, rocks, and islands are easily identified as Lismer's. The cartoons are informal and amusing records of family events. Less known are those he drew for his own entertainment, as he experimented with lines and ideas.

The section titles have been chosen from those my father gave to his paintings. They have the poetic quality apparent in all his writing. Here, however, it may be best not to look for any special relationship between text and title.

In 1945 my father wrote an autobiography intended as information for a script in a radio series on Canadian painters. This manuscript forms the first chapter of the present study. Whenever it was appropriate, additional notes or portions of letters have been inserted into the text. For instance, when Lismer mentioned his first trip to Algonquin Park his description has been expanded with notes on his first impressions, written immediately after that visit.

> "They took life seriously, art lightly, and their Canadianism strenuously, but were blithely unconcious of anything in the way of making history. It can truly be said now that we all believed in the other fellow and were not very conscious of ourselves as a movement or having any particular niche to fill in Canada's edifice."

When someone, making polite conversation perhaps, asks me how it was to grow up in the 'stimulating atmosphere generated by the Group of Seven' I have to admit that I do not know. I was too young to be concerned. If there were lively discussions, I did not listen. As I look back on those days, life seems to have been normal and peaceful. I begin to wonder, then, what I do remember about my father. The public image is unclear. Until the late twenties I gave it very little thought; after the mid-thirties I was no longer at home. I was then living in the United States and Canadian art news was scarce. In my father's infrequent letters he did not say much about himself.

This sounds as if he were a vague and remote figure to his family. Not true, however. I think that he tended to keep the two aspects of his life, the public and the private, separated as much as possible. Of course, there were many friends who touched both parts, and many overlapping activities. But home was a place for resting and relaxing and my mother did her best to protect him from intrusion. In a letter to his sister in England Dad once wrote, "Life is sweet and serene in our home." For him, it was a refuge.

4

Penguins, Vancouver Zoo (undated)

Even if the public figure is vague, there is no doubt that the man who was my father was close and real. This is the person I associate with our leisure time and vacations. Both were certainly family affairs. Holiday time did not mean inactivity. But it brought about a change of pace — a slowing down, a relaxation of all the city pressures. He lingered over meals, generally took a nap in the afternoon, read detective stories, and sketched as the mood struck him.

Our vacations stretched all over Canada. These must also include the summers spent in England and Europe, and the months we lived in South Africa, Australia, and New Zealand. These trips were busy ones for my father. They should, however, fall into the category of 'vacations' in the sense that they were away from the routine pressures of our normal life and in an unfamiliar environment. This developed a special closeness for the three of us, and we shared many activities. It is under these circumstances that I best remember him.

M.L.B.

Fox's Farm, England, 1900

One   Road Through the Bush

Arthur Lismer's brief introduction to his autobiography tells us that it was written, 'not as a record of achievement, but as the experience of an artist who came from an old land, and found new life in a new environment.'

Around Sheffield, where I was born in 1885, the countryside has a noble beauty of its own — great expanses of moorland and upland farm country, where the magic light and shadow play a dramatic melody of colour, weather, and pattern. The towns are ugly and in the city of Sheffield a heavy pall of smoke from the countless blast furnaces hangs over the grey, dark buildings, and the skyline is serrated with tall chimneys and huge factories. It is a prosperous and vital centre of heavy trades and finely tempered cutlery, famous the world over. It lies in a lovely frame, like a smoky, sullen stone in a gloriously designed setting. It is surrounded by the hills, woods, and dales of Yorkshire and Derbyshire, with the craggy silhouettes of the typical north country of England.

Its people are hospitable, stubborn, non-conformist folk, with a fine sense of stern duty to their vocations and their interests in music, poetry, and the arts. Yorkshire men and women are scattered far over the British Empire — clanny folk, speaking a rugged dialect, unmistakable, and sometimes un-English in sound. Yorkshire people have a passion for education and travel, and able hands for the making of fine objects.

It is the environment that, for me, played a strong and memorable part in the early experience of getting to know the why and the wherefore about drawing and painting. As far back as I can recall I was always drawing, filling innumerable sketchbooks with drawings of farms, trees, and people.

When I was twelve years of age I saw a notice in the local newspaper that the South Riding County authorities were offering scholarships to young artists to the local School of Art. I presented myself for examination, and one day received notice that I was one of the twelve in the district awarded a seven-year scholarship. That seemed to settle it. My people were by no means well off. My father was a working man with a large family, and no doubt an artist in the family was a trial. But I had to work at some trade, and at thirteen years of age I was apprenticed to a photo-engraving firm attached to the local newspaper. I served the full period of seven years articled to the business, or profession, of a black-and-white artist. At fifteen years of age I was doing cartoons, courtroom scenes, 'the spot where the body was found', and the festivals, royal visits, football matches, and so on of a great manufacturing city.

At the same time I worked at the Art School five nights a week, and went the full length of my scholarship. On week-ends we roamed the countryside on sketching 'forays'. We banded into small clubs and occasionally had a minor effort exhibited in the local art show. The instruction at the Art School was arid, academic, and devoid of inspiration — historical ornament, cast drawing, and (drawing) from life. All colourless, stern, and unimaginative. But it must have had some value, in a disciplinary way, and I must have been amenable, and even ambitious. At twenty I had a diploma and I was free from my apprenticeship. I took my very small savings to Antwerp, in Belgium, across the grey North Sea, where I spent a year or so, drawing continuously and mixing with the life of a great port and the picturesque 'continental' environment of a strange assortment of cathedrals, narrow streets, shipping, canals, art galleries, and museums.

Incidentally, we did not pay a cent for instruction in Antwerp, and this was over forty years ago. Today (1945) in this country, there are few places where a young artist, whether he is a foreigner or not, can get free education in art for as long as he needs it, and under governmental sponsorship.

I visited Holland and France and returned home penniless with no attractive future. It was a cold world for artists in those days in northern England. In January, 1911, I sailed for Canada on the old Cunarder, the *Corsican,* with few dollars and high hopes. We landed at Halifax after a wintery storm at sea, making a picturesque entry with the ship encased in ice from 'truck to keelson'. Making for Toronto the next day through the winter landscape, snowbound for a day or two in the Matapedia Valley, hearing about Canadian history from a little French priest and about the woods from a lumberman, wondering where the cities were in this vast country, and seeing green skies, purple shadows and spruce bush — these are among my recollections.

I found a job in a lithographing firm, and later joined the *Grip Engraving Company* as a commercial artist. Here I met people who became my friends. There was Tom McLean who knew the northern woods and lakes; Jim Mac-Donald, a Northumbrian with the face of a priest and the soul of a poet; Frank Carmichael, Frank Johnston, Albert Robson, and others. There was Tom Thomson, who did fine lettering and layouts for advertising, and dreamed of the North Country. He had not yet put brush to canvas or panel; and Varley, who joined us later in 1912. There were sketching excursions into the surrounding country — up the Humber or Don River in York county — all Yorkshire names. I felt at home.

Edward Lismer, 1910

From this coterie of fellow-workers came, eventually, the beginnings of the Group of Seven.

I returned to England in May, 1912, spent a honeymoon in Belgium, and returned to Canada in August of the same year. I gave up my job in commercial art at *Grip's* and went out on my own as a free-lance illustrator. I did badly, earning a meager living doing advertising chores — and I disliked it intensely. In fact, I disliked the advertising profession completely, although I remember it was at that time on a higher level than was general in England. I wanted to paint. I sold my first painting, purchased by the Ontario Government, in 1913. That was the same exhibition (the *Ontario Society of Artists'* annual show, at the Public Library on College Street, Toronto) at which Tom Thomson sold **his** first picture. He cashed his cheque in dollar bills and grub-staked another trip up North. I bought a cot and a baby carriage with the proceeds of my first sale.

My first trip to Algonquin Park was in May 1914. I met Thomson at Canoe Lake Station. I still remember the cold spring night, the piping of young frogs, and the drive through the bush to Fraser's. Thomson introduced me to the wonders of the North Country. I learned to see the trails, to paddle a canoe, make camp, and to catch fish. I learned to see Canada in its rugged beauty and design. We portaged and sketched. We moved over this magic land of Algonquin Park, from one lake to another, and I trod with Thomson on old trails with the snow yet lying in the recesses of the thick bush — and I saw the birch burst into vibrant yellow-green overnight — saw the haunts of the beaver and heard the cry of the Canada goose heading still northward. My first real thrill of sketching in Canada and learning to love it was at this time.

More than thirty years before this was written, Lismer had already recorded his first impressions of Algonquin Park, only a week or so after his return from the sketching trip with Thomson. Both descriptions, in spite of the years between, reveal the same wonder and excitement, and a love for the North Country that stayed with him all his life.

We were there in a wonderful time, when everything was on the very edge of rebirth. It was very cold in the evenings, and the temperature about midnight and up to the early morning was below the freezing point. Any water left in the pails around the camp was frozen hard. But the sun came up and everything responded to its glow and warmth.... We were sleeping in an open tent, with one pair of blankets, and never once did we feel the cold. We were, indeed, too healthily tired after our days in the open to think about it.

The North has an atmosphere and a glamour all its own. I have never experienced anything like it anywhere else — it is peculiarly of this North Country and I can't describe it. The first night when I arrived the whole feeling burst upon me at once. I reached Canoe Lake about ten o'clock in the evening after a stuffy nine hours in the train. I was met by Thomson who had brought down the wagon and we drove through the bush to where he was staying. Imagine a glorious moon coming over the tops of the spruce, big and yellow, shedding a mysterious light on everything. The air had a tang of freshness and cold that was wonderfully invigorating and refreshing after the stuffy train and the city I had left. One smelt the trees and the fragrance of the ground beneath, and the moonlight had colour — you could see to paint and be able to appreciate the colour of things. This was the background and setting, as it were, to a wonderful chorus of sounds — the night chorus of nature's orchestra — the wind in the pines — the shrill cry of the loons — the never-ending piping of innumerable frogs and toads rising and falling in rhythmical cadence, the low booming of the bittern, the hooting of owls. I felt I longed to be in tune with it all. I wanted to find something in myself, some forgotten, latent chord was touched. I felt happy, exalted, and indescribably out-of-tune — satiated with city life and all the petty accumulations of busy days which meant nothing. That first impression was wonderfully helpful. It was greater than imagination, charged with meaning and growth to an impressionable soul, a quickening of feeling, the birth of new impulses and outlooks, and an intense desire to express it.

We stayed overnight at Fraser's, Canoe Lake, and pulled out the next forenoon. Our canoe was a sixteen-foot Chestnut, canvas covered, roomy and capable of carrying the weight we had to put in it — stores for two weeks, tents, blankets, a cooking stove and utensils, plates and pannikins of aluminum, fishing tackle, axe, and sketching impedimenta. I had two dozen 12 x 9 three-ply veneer boards of birch wood with soft pine inside. These fitted into a holder designed to carry six, and two more in a flat sketch box; also about twelve to fifteen pounds of paint, oil and brushes....

I can hardly describe spring in the maple bush. It is one of the wonders of God's creation — the tall sombre trunks purply grey, and delicate branches in-

*Thomson and Robson at Grip
Engraving, Toronto, 1911*

terwoven in a marvelous intricacy of pattern, each little twig alive with dancing buds, some scarlet, some brown and yellow, and with the sun shining through and repeating, with new delicacy, their shadows on the thick carpet of fallen leaves of the previous fall through which the spring flowers were forcing their way — the song of the thrasher, the trilling notes of the oriole, and the powerful hammering of a huge hammer-headed woodpecker.

Everything was growing, growing, growing — everything had a song. Never have I appreciated the big idea of Spring before so strongly. There — a contrast in the depth of cedar grove, or pines and spruce bush — here — a merciless tangle of fallen trees and age-long struggle with the elements. Wind and fire have swept it, and thick and soft beneath the feet is a deep, springy carpet of needles from the evergreens, in which no green thing grows. Overhead, the heavy interlacing branches permit but little light to penetrate. Only here and there a shaft of light has caught the top of a rotting stump, and burns like a sacrificial fire in some huge primeval temple.

It is significant that at this first meeting with the Canadian bush Lismer was immediately intrigued with all the small and close-up details. His description of the interior of the forest is much like his later paintings, such as *Sunlight in a Wood,* or the twisted growth in *Canadian Jungle,* and the many woodland studies from British Columbia. Apparently he was not yet ready for his later approach to the landscape.

In the summer of 1915 I started to teach at the Ontario College of Art Teacher Training Courses. In 1916 I went to Halifax as Principal of the Nova Scotia College of Art (then the Victoria School of Art and Design). I stayed there for three years. It was an old established school, in a decrepit building, even then. There were no pupils and I had to go out and find them. That first year we formed 'teen-age classes for children of the Halifax schools, and commenced to build up the enrolment. By the second year we had small but well established courses. In 1917 the great Halifax explosion shattered the school and we had to close down for a spell. But for two years after, it continued to grow, and when I left in 1919 I was wiser in experience, and knew more about teaching and about young people.

Treetops, Georgian Bay, (undated)

Oak Leaves (undated)

Antwerp, 1908

·With·all·good·wishes·
·for·a·happy·
·Christmas·&·
·a·Bright·New·Year·

·with·love·
·from·
·Arthur·

Christmas
1908.

African Craftsmen, 1936

Roy Mitchell, Hart House Theatre, Toronto, 1920

While in Halifax I made War Records of naval activities. I went out to sea with convoys, in minesweepers and submarine chasers, and sketched fortifications and guns. I saw the huge ships come home in 1919 with Canadians who had fought in the Great War of 1914 - 1918. It was in Nova Scotia that I found a love of sea and sea coast, ships and fishing gear, and that most wonderful province.

Life in Nova Scotia was pleasant, in spite of wartime restrictions. We rented a small house in Bedford, right at the head of Bedford Basin, at the mouth of the Sackville River. There was about an acre of ground — all of it on a hillside. In summer there were picnics, boating, and swimming. In winter the snow was thick on the ground and my father bought a sled big enough to hold us both. We went skimming down our hillside road to the edge of the frozen water. In spring the logs came down the river to be caught in booms. The men worked frantically to keep the logs moving in the river and to untangle the log-jams that developed at a moment's notice. There are a number of Lismer sketches and drawings of this activity.

The Halifax explosion in December, 1917, was a great disaster for that city. But our family's personal involvement was minor. Contrary to newspaper accounts at that time, my father did **not** miss his usual train into town that morning. Because of his Saturday morning classes he generally kept a free day during the week. On this particular morning he had had no plans to go to work. We had not yet had breakfast when we heard the noise and saw the smoke in the distance. In our house, nearly twelve miles from the disaster, the damage was not serious — soot all over the breakfast table and a number of shattered windows.

In June, 1918, Eric Brown of the National Gallery in Ottawa asked Lismer if he would make drawings of harbour and shipping activities for the Canadian War Records. Commissions were not given for specific pictures, but rather a free hand to collect material for later development and possible purchase by the National Gallery. Because my father had had previous experience with lithography he chose this as a means for recording the drama of ships and planes and men at war.

In later years my father returned many times to Nova Scotia. I believe it was second only to Georgian Bay as a favorite sketching ground. The combination of rocks and peaceful inlets, littered docks and old fish houses, made Nova Scotia fascinating.

I returned to Toronto in September, 1919, was appointed Vice-Principal of the Ontario College of Art, and commenced again to find a way to teach and to organize a school of art. We started young people's classes on Saturday mornings for Toronto school children. During the period from 1919 to 1927 I taught steadily — having to make a decision between the life of a painter and that of a teacher. I managed to do both. It was during these years that the Art Gallery of Toronto was beginning to build its new galleries; the Group of Seven was founded; Hart House, University of Toronto was opened. Our early experiments in the theatre arts, with the late Roy Mitchell as leader, commenced in Hart House.

My vacations were few, but whenever possible I went with my wife and family up to Georgian Bay — sometimes with Jackson, MacDonald, or Varley. At first it was to Go Home Bay, then further north to McGregor Bay, near Manitoulin Island. Georgian Bay! Thousands of islands, little and big, some of them mere rocks just breaking the surface of the waters of the Bay — others with great, high rocks tumbled in confused masses and crowned with leaning pines, turned away in ragged disarray from the west wind, presenting a strange pattern against the sky and water. Some of the trees are like miniatures in an oriental garden, their roots seeking tenacious hold in the cracks in the rocks. The undergrowth is tangled and in spring the wild iris and cherry blossoms cluster round little pools in the hollows.

At the time of the equinoxial gales the aspect changes — the waters storm in great waves, beating against the outer islands and the sky is a stormy pattern of cloudrack scudding across the horizon. I painted *September Gale*, which is in the National Gallery at Ottawa, during one of these storms. In winter the frozen water and snow-clad islands give the whole district a remote and lonely aspect — beautiful, rhythmic, and sombre, like a Chinese painting. Georgian Bay — the happy isles, all different, but bound together in a common unity of form, colour, and design. It is a paradise for painters.

During those years, and until 1932, I was Principal of Teacher Training in Art for the Ontario Government Summer Courses, and Vice-Principal of the Ontario College of Art until 1927, when I became Educational Supervisor at the Art Gallery of Toronto, organizing public programmes for children and adults. These were exciting years, and the real beginning of my work on Saturday mornings for young children from eight years to twelve. We organized these classes for all who wanted to come. In the next two years we had five hundred students, transforming the quiet galleries with sights and sounds of activity, with children working at

painting and drawing in all the galleries. I don't know how many tons of paper, pencils, colour, clay, and other materials we used, or just how many young and enthusiastic teachers we had — all of whom were my associates in the common task of releasing child expression in the arts.

Toronto was the centre of this movement, which has spread to other Canadian cities, and to other countries. The Carnegie Corporation (of New York) endowed our work with liberal grants, without which the effort would have been impossible. In 1932 we started the Children's Art Centre, near the Art Gallery of Toronto. Here the study of childhood through art began — experimental, intensified, and with regard to personality and character of childhood. We looked at life through a child's eye and found much that education in schools had ignored. A famous Austrian educator, Franz Cizek, said, "There is much of autumn and winter in life, but spring never comes again." He was the pioneer of our day in the recognition of the child as artist. It was always springtime at the Children's Art Centre, in Grange Park.

In 1932 I went to France, Italy, and England lecturing in these countries on art and child education. I toured Italy with a group of people. Possibly this was the first Art Appreciation tour for Canadians ever in Europe.

From 1932 to 1939 I made several lecture tours across Canada, from Vancouver Island to Halifax. In Ontario I travelled north, east, and west with a box of slides and a lantern, talking about education and painting, in all sorts of places. It was on these trips that I learned to know that all racial types, people, communities were linked together by one common denominator — art, the love of created things and the desire towards expression in some form of artistic effort. It is the emotional ally of intelligence and desire to mould, to illustrate, and to make personal contributions to the age-long yearnings for humanity to enliven and decorate the fringe of laborious life with a border of beauty.

Algonquin Park, 1914

31

Community art is no new thing for Canada. It is always there. There have always been people, whether children or grown-ups, who came together in welfare associations, libraries, settlements, and in remote places where the official hand of government or chartered associations has never reached. In music, drama, and the crafts there are teachers who have the love of community in their hearts. They bring groups together to express the deep sentiments of peaceful people. Such things as differences in race, creed, and language are secondary to the common language of art in action. In these things lie the hope for Canadian childhood and our future as a nation of those who appreciate beauty by doing something about it themselves.

In the Art Gallery of Toronto, as part of our educational programme, we introduced many new features to attract people, and to remove the pedestal-gazing aspect of art. We had music, plays, pageants, dances related to some particular people or period on view in the changing exhibitions on the walls. The mausoleum gloom of the average Art Gallery was dissipated and thousands actually came to enjoy art. Canada has at least done **that** job — removing the awe from the public Art Gallery. Toronto was the pioneer city in this movement. It was the children who led the parents into the sacred precincts, sharing the keys and opening the doors to the treasure houses. Public education in the schools changed and other galleries opened up children's classes. Now it has become commonplace, and nobody wonders any longer at what children can do with paint and clay, or what galleries and museums (can) present in the way of entertainment and instruction, in addition to permanent collections and annual exhibitions. Aquisition is not everything. This is the age of distribution.

Our exhibitions of Child-Art were going out to all countries, to England, France, United States, Japan and Latin America. In 1934 I made my first trip to South Africa, under the auspices of the Carnegie Corporation. My family and I left Toronto (and I shall never forget the crowds of children and teachers who saw us off) for England and then to Cape Town. With us went a large exhibition of Canadian children's drawings and paintings. We visited many cities in the Union of South Africa, lecturing in Cape Town, Johannesburg, Durban. We saw something of Zululand and lectured to coloured teachers; and in the various universities (spoke) to thousands of white teachers. It was almost as if they had never heard about art, or Canada, or children. This experience was introductory, for we went back again in 1936.

An interest in Art, 1932

In the years between 1934 and 1937 the Lismer family made several lengthy sea voyages. All three of us were good sailors and greatly enjoyed the life aboard an ocean liner. In those days the sea trip from Southhampton to Cape Town, South Africa, took seventeen days. The weather was generally good, and life was slow and relaxing. My father liked this life. He and mother walked the decks, played deck games together, and sat reading in some sheltered corner. Every afternoon he took a nap, waking in time for tea. Although friendly with their neighbours on deck or in the lounge, they did not join in the communal activities, except as spectators. My father, however, was called upon to judge the costumes at the usual fancy dress ball.

His restless pencil was constantly in his hand. He never went anywhere without drawing material in his pocket. Whenever he sketched he usually had a group of people watching over his shoulder, but this never seemed to bother him, and he would carry on a conversation as he worked. He was impatient waiting for mealtime service in the ship's dining salon, or in restaurants anywhere, and he spent the time drawing on menu cards, table napkins, placemats — anything that came to hand. To my mother's horror, he would even draw on the plates, and then quickly wipe them off with a table napkin when she protested. In any ship or hotel dining room the drawings would be snatched up by the waiters and the diners. Some were even taken back to the chef in the kitchen. There must be Lismer drawings in every corner of the British Commonwealth and the U.S.A. Wherever he was, he illustrated the daily activities, or an item on the menu, or the group at the next table. He never seemed to stop drawing. If he was writing a report he doodled in the margins. If he was reading a paperback book he drew in the blank spaces. He also illustrated his personal letters and his crossword puzzle books — all with swift, expressive lines:

In the year 1936 I really started travelling. I returned to South Africa, this time at the invitation of the South African Government. We were there for a year, spending a few months in different centres of the Union. We went first to Johannesburg, and then up into the British Protectorate of Bechuanaland somewhere on the fringe of the Kalahari Desert and three hundred miles north of Mafeking. There we established the first native Art Centre in South Africa.

For many days I met black people who came long, weary miles across country — native chiefs, teachers in native schools, craftsmen, potters and carvers. We talked about art and children, sometimes out in the open in the shadow of a great fig tree, and at other times in the village school at the mission station. This **was** an experience — telling them about the children in Canada and showing their drawings, and having them draw for us. How they sang and danced! Their smiles and their gratitude were infectious. I learned that little black children had personalities and clever hands.

I recall visiting a native school, telling them a story of giants and, getting permission to draw on the white wall, I drew a huge giant and a beanstalk, and a native hut far below and the distant mountains of their own country that they knew. They laughed and cried with pleasure and I guess **that** wall has not been re-whitewashed since that day.

After that I spent many weeks in Basutoland, Zululand, and other native territories, staying in missions and native houses, driving long hours over vast plains with wild game in the distance, and at night the call of strange birds and beasts. This land is so unlike anything in Canada. South Africa is not a dark continent. For the eye, it is a constant feast of light; golden colour and purple distance. A field of green shines, like a jewel, from some patch of field crop. One misses the keen blue sky and the luscious greens of summer, but the new features of teeming life, animal and human, in the native places, are unbelievably fascinating.

In the universities and training centres for white people in the big towns, we formed art groups and training classes for children. On the high veld, in mining centres, in farming districts, in small settlements and big ones I lectured and showed slides and moving pictures, and children's drawings. Today there are Children's Art Centres in different parts of South Africa, and there are more intelligent attitudes to art education in the schools.

In 1937 we went from there to Australia, across the south Indian Ocean — from Perth to Brisbane, from Melbourne to Tasmania, and from Sydney to New Zealand. I saw Art Galleries and Museums, and schools and more schools. The children sang, drew pictures, and danced for us in all these places. I could tell you of strange places where only Maoris went to school and when I asked them what I should draw they cried out with one voice — what do you think — COWBOYS! Tasmania, what a lovely fertile land; Melbourne, a beautiful city; Sydney, its marvelous harbour; Rotorua, the thermal region of New Zealand; the cattle country of South Island, and the great mountains. On the way home, I lectured in Fiji to fuzzy-haired people at school in the hills.

Peggy's Cove, Nova Scotia, 1930   *Georgian Bay Pines (undated)*

This may have nothing to do with Canadian painting. It merely gives spice to the routine of a year and a half of travel and hard work in many new lands. I came back with one big idea, at least — that people everywhere were peaceful, happy, and agreeable to each other, and children were eager to know about other children. Colour and language made little difference. When we learn about them and know them better we cannot hate nor look down upon them. They are just like ourselves, but in a different setting, and that goes for grown-ups as well. When we seek child nature we discover the true artist and the real human, with no inhibitions, no hatreds, and no lack of courage in expression. If released, it unfolds a thousand new aspects of character that art alone can reveal. Childhood is real and is something in its own right, with its own world, and not, in any way, an adult world.

When I returned to Canada in September, 1937, I came back to a changing scene. The children's classes and the Children's Art Centre were firmly established. My staff had done nobly in my absence. I sent off one of my associates (Miss Norah McCullough) to South Africa and through her efforts the South African Children's Art Centres have been established.

In the summer of 1938 I lectured in Hawaii, and spent a month in that delightful island. In Honolulu there was a mixed audience of children under a banyan tree, all wanting to draw and paint, just because somebody was showing them that they could do it for themselves. There was a Samoan wedding and a wild dance with swords, a feast of roast pig cooked in the sand, and a thousand baffling odours and tastes.

Then I came back to Toronto, only to leave again. This time I was really emigrating to the U.S.A., with an appointment as Professor of Fine Arts at Columbia University Teachers College.

He did not really want to go to the States. As far back as August, 1935, the National Gallery had suggested the possibility of Lismer working in Ottawa after his return from the tour of the Southern Dominions. It was then a tentative approach, but well received on all sides — by my father, the National Gallery, and the Carnegie Corporation of New York, which would provide financial support. This would give him an opportunity to expand his work with children on a national scale. But after his return to Toronto, when nothing certain could be expected from the National Gallery, although he waited until the last minute, he accepted the invitation from

41

Teachers College. In October 1938, from his apartment in New York, he wrote to Dr. Frederick Keppel of the Carnegie Corporation. This was a man my father regarded as a warm friend and a wise counselor:

> I have not troubled you much with details about my leaving Toronto, and accepting the position here in T.C. (Teachers College). But I am rather dismayed to find that McCurry believes that he has been basely deceived and that he has you now 'on the spot'. I have had a letter from him in which he outlines his opinions about my defection from Canada and my duties and responsibilities to the National Gallery in particular. He is an old friend — and I can discount a lot of it, but at the same time I can't let him get away with this idea that any other person decided for me what I should do.
>
> It is a long story and I left Canada in a very bitter mood. I did not want to come to New York; but when one after another of my plans came unstuck, and finally at the last moment, when my own decision had to be made with the Dean of T.C., Ottawa had no plan, no promise, except a vague something that I should go to the National Gallery and do a sort of promotion job for the good of the National Gallery's soul. I opened out my plan at their offer in April last, and nothing matured or developed during the interim, up to July 15th, to reassure me that I could set up my staff and my work in a new and national environment in Ottawa.

He and my Mother settled down in New York, somewhat surprised at finding themselves there. They enjoyed the many galleries and museums, the parks and gardens of the city, and were contented enough for the time being. Shortly after his arrival my father wrote to friends in Toronto about his first impressions of life in New York City:

> It seems strange to me that I should be sitting in an apartment about eight stories above the pavement, on the heights of Columbia, putting down my impressions of New York. First of all, it is not the kind of job that I like. I like people and children, and things in streets, houses, parks, and life stirring. I don't like stagnant things and sentiments you have to dig for, and blast a way through resistance and evasions. I like growing things, buds and little trees, pups and shells. I like spring more than fall — dawn and twilight rather than the glare of noonday sun, full summer, and limelight. There is always a feeling in Canada that things are moving and growing, design and life forming. There is that here, of course, but it is more finished, more accomplished, and the kind of action and

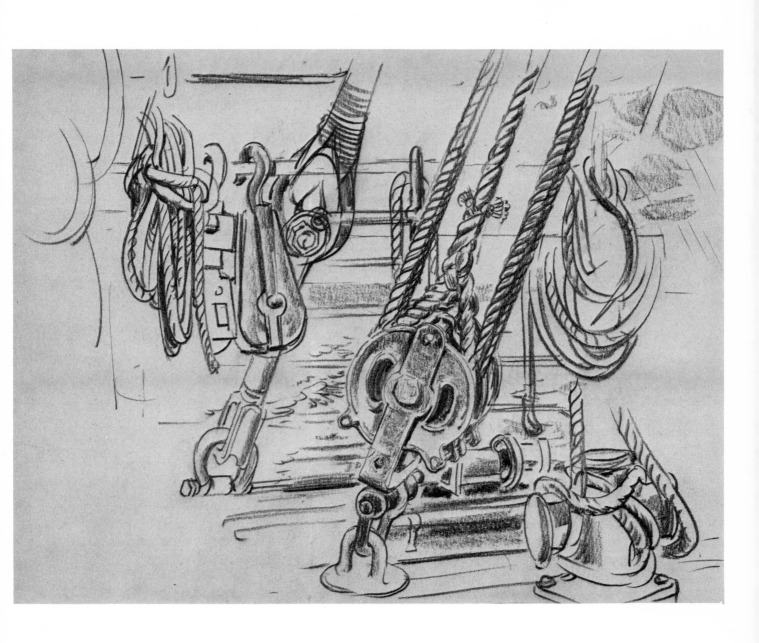

Ropes and Pulleys, 1930's

movement around is more the erratic hurrying of ants that one sees when the top of their little earth world is kicked aside.

New York is like that. The people, surrounded by marvels of architecture and exciting vistas, museums, and things to contemplate, seem to be forever hurrying on foolish errands of high importance. They have tight and anxious masks of concentration on their shoulders. Then they talk and write, and tell everyone, and record their impressions, and irritations, and difficulties about a momentuous experience of — (well) probably buying a bottle of perfume at Woolworth's or a percolator at Macy's. They don't let the world go by and enjoy it. They go by the world and wait for it to catch up.

They are a marvelous people, taking for granted that all the good things around them, that come from civic enterprise, private effort, and the grace of God, are theirs by the democratic right of all men to share the riches of everybody.... We in Canada are amateurs in the science of efficient living and we have a lot to learn. We know nothing, comparatively about short cuts and mechanized emotions, where everything can be put on a bottle label — where vitamins and panaceas, highways and engineering, neuroses and psychoses, ailments and emotions can be docketed and tagged, pigeon-holed and cross-indexed for everybody's use.

Education is included in this, and education can be a terribly efficient activity, leaving no room for doubt or imagination. 'If it moves, we can educate it. If it is alive, we can keep it moving.' I have been sitting in with a distinguished gang of educators — or should I say with a gang of distinguished educators? They make me feel old and mature. Then I begin to feel as if I know nothing at all about the machinery of education, or about work-plans and time-rhythms, and sentiments about everything. They **know** so darned much about more and more, and they feel so little about less and less. I want to get my pick into their statistical exteriors and find the real man inside.... These people know so much about how the mind works that they do not stop to contemplate what it works **on.** Contemplation is apparently a weakness. The written, legalized, sanitized, documentary evidence and proof is what they want and they know how to get it — and quickly, too.

This is an exaggeration, of course, and quite possibly it **is** a sign of youth and energy. But certainly living in a country where every road is mapped out for them, and where the sky in the city is something above the houses, and the green parks are where the children play in safety, and entertainment is for leisure only, and all games are officially circumscribed by rules and scientifically organized to keep one fit for business — living in such a country is in itself a form of adventurous participation in everyone's business except one's own.

I lectured in many places, east and west in the United States. I conducted courses in Child Art and Teacher Training at Columbia. We were settled there for good, I believed. The nostalgic glances backwards to Canada, and the pull of such places as Georgian Bay and the Maritimes to bring one back, were too strong, and I returned, after a year, to the National Gallery in Ottawa, to establish a National Art Centre. The funds were there and the hopes were high, but the war started in 1939, and these were never realized.

Although he learned a great deal from his year's association with American educational methods, Lismer was glad to return to Canada. He had written an astute and comprehensive report on the state of art education in New York. Its recommendations had been politely accepted. Nevertheless, he was convinced that his work would now find a place on a shelf somewhere, and soon be forgotten.

After spending a short holiday in Cape Cod and then in Georgian Bay, my parents moved to Ottawa in August. But the situation continued to be confused and Lismer felt he was taking his salary under false pretenses. Writing to Dr. Keppel he said, "Up to the present, my position has been one of amiable insecurity. I have been treated well as a visiting artist, pleasant but humiliating." After a year of this uncertainty he was happy to accept an invitation from the Montreal Art Association (now the Montreal Museum of Fine Arts).

My personal reaction to the National Gallery scheme is that he was well out of it. It is impossible to fit my father into the conventional picture of the Civil Servant (with capitals). His mind required immediate reaction to new ideas from a lively and responsive staff. He would not willingly accept long delays, nor the constant exercise of patience and tact, necessary when dealing with governmental bureaucracy. He was depressed by the apathy of uninformed and uncaring officials. The year that he spent in Ottawa, trying to organize the National Art Centre, was probably the most frustrating of his whole life. Mr. H.O. McCurry, who was then the Director of the National Gallery, knew my father well and could foresee some of the difficulties ahead. But he, on his part, could have been more tactful when he wrote in a postscript to a letter to Lismer, "We expect you to be an asset to the hard-pressed National Gallery — not a liability."

Quebec Barns, 1925

In December of 1940 I came to Montreal and started all over again, organizing an Art Gallery and Museum into educational activity with children and adults. By this time the pattern was evident. I knew what would happen, and it did. Teachers, children, French and English speaking, came. (There were) activities of lecturing, instructing, school visits, children's classes, and the Art School (of the Montreal Art Association) to revive.

Montreal is an exciting place, with its racial impacts and factions, and high emotional activity in the arts. We have now (1945) about three hundred children in the classes, from three years to fourteen, and over five hundred adult students in the Art School. I am on the staff of McGill University, lecturing in Aesthetics and Art History. I conduct a course in art for 'non-professional' business men and women, and now, after five years of activity of this kind, we are to open a new Children's Art Centre in Montreal.

In these years I have managed to paint a lot of pictures — a few good, many very ordinary. I have been back to Georgian Bay and the Maritimes. All I can say of my present work is that it is more active than ever and that I have a large staff of experienced workers. I still have pictures to paint and ideas about travel and education, and memories of pioneering in strange places in far lands — which I occasionally visit in recollection of people young and old. Then I wonder why we have war. If people were busy creating things they would have no time for destruction and hatred — and we should not indoctrinate for anything, but let human beings grow naturally — in a land where the chief vital nourishment is their sustaining and natural art, that is ours to discover and release.

The autobiography ends with 1945. There was still nearly a quarter of a century of hard and rewarding work ahead, at least twenty of these years with undiminished vigor. Dr. Martin, of the Montreal Art Association, in a letter to Dr. Keppel in New York reported that Lismer had said he was 'never happier'. The years in Montreal seem to have been peaceful ones. There were controversies and disappointments, but not the turmoil of the decades in Toronto. The Group of Seven had now become 'old hat', as Lismer frequently noted, pointing out that this was as it should be. My father was always interested in what was ahead and he seldom talked about the past. He preferred to look to the future.

In the next twenty-five years many public distinctions came to him. Both Dalhousie University in the Maritimes and McGill in Montreal conferred honorary degrees upon him. He was pleased, impressed, and embarrassed, in turn. These were honours he seemed to accept as impersonal, not given to **him**, but an expression of the value of the work itself. He had other awards — the Canada Council Medal in 1963, the Centennial Medal in 1967, and highest of all, Companion of Canada, also in 1967. I suspect the honour that gave him the greatest amusement was a routine one from the Royal Canadian Academy. In 1957 the former rebel painter became a Senior Academician.

He retained his position as Principal of the Art School, in the Montreal Museum of Fine Arts, until 1967. At that time he became Principal Emeritus. He had already retired from his position as Professor of Fine Arts at McGill. He was unhappy at the closing down of his activities, and even at 82 he was not ready to let go. To him, his mind and his skills were as acute as ever. But there was no doubt that his memory was becoming unreliable. The habit of years, however, was too strong to curtail abruptly. He continued to walk to the Museum almost every day. Because they held him in respect and affection the staff of the Museum accepted this.

After he died in March, 1969, there were many tributes in the newspapers across Canada. The one that touched me most deeply, and expressed my father's spirit best, appeared as an editorial in the Montreal Gazette on March 27th:

> Sherbrooke Street will never seem quite the same again, now that Dr. Lismer is gone. Every day, and in all sorts of weather, he was to be seen striding along, with his beloved and battered hat, and his long white hair, his cheerful, humorous face, and a pipe in his mouth.
>
> He was more than a picturesque figure. Of him it could be said that he had 'entered into the immortality of his fame while still among his countrymen.'
>
> Those who saw Dr. Lismer walking by were looking upon a figure out of the history of Canadian art. He had been an original member of the Group of Seven, the small band of determined artists who transformed Canadian art and gave the country an artistic consciousness. However much art has changed, and may change, the place and importance of the Group of Seven are secure.

50

Arthur Lismer was in it from the start of the Group of Seven, as they explored the country around Georgian Bay and found new loveliness in weather-beaten rocks and crooked trees bent by the storms.

It might seem strange that a man of Dr. Lismer's talents as a painter should have spent so much of his time as a teacher. It was not mere necessity; he loved it. For him art was not only a craft to be learned by the few, but something for everybody, as natural as living. That was why he spent so much of his later years teaching art to children, or rather, helping them to express themselves in art. He was convinced that 'the artist can never recapture the speed and spontaneity of childhood.'

And Dr. Lismer was one of the last of the happy artists. Not for him was the modern gloom, and introspection, and savagery, and complaints and despair. For him it was as good to paint and draw as it was to be alive. He was too vital to be a pessimist. He urged everyone to 'glance around to see the beauty of the new experiences being unfolded in our passage through life.'

He passed through a long life, leaving it fresher and clearer, as with the passing of a September gale.

Two   The Happy Isles

If Arthur Lismer had been free to wander the length and breadth of Canada, as A.Y. Jackson did, he would have thoroughly enjoyed the adventure. But I believe he would still have preferred the intimate subject matter of Georgian Bay and the Maritimes, or the woods and beaches of Vancouver Island. He was probably least attracted to the long vistas of the prairies and the vastness of the mountains. These were picturesque in their own way, but to him they were not as interesting to paint. He recognized the great variety within Canada, each area unique, waiting for someone to interpret it. My father, however, wanted to get close to his material. More and more he concentrated on the foreground; and in later years frequently ignored even the middle distance. He wrote in 1929:

> We have a background of epic grandeur. Vast areas of lake and bush, pastoral country of great beauty, and wide prairie lands — monotonous, fruitful, and strongly alluring — mountains and foothills, seaports and inland seas.... It is a land where romance and rugged charm lie, not in resemblance to another country, but in their own significant forms of beauty and colour. Twisted and gnarled pines and space illimitable, backwater and beaver meadows, swirling rapids, placid lakes and hardwood bush, jack pine and spruce, red maple, tamarack and cedar — all these are motives that make Canada distinctive. There is little of pictorial finish and mere pastoral sweetness, nothing finished to copy, little enticement for the seeker of conventional prettiness.
>
> The seasons are not the same. There is no soft gliding of winter into spring. The hillside of birch that was a grey, shimmering purple in the evening of one day is a mass of vibrant yellow-green foliage the next, and the waters of the lake are powdered with the golden dust of its birth. The poplar in the fall, a golden glory of yellow in the early morning sun, after a night of frost, will shed all its leaves in an instantaneous shower at the first breath of wind from the lake, like a terrier shaking its coat free of water.
>
> The procession of the months is a chromatic joy. Spring with its fresh, quick greens, and yellow flowers; summer — hot dense foliage of blue-greens and bronze, vibrant and lighter in hue than in an English summer. The fall (comes) with such an amazing pageantry of warmth of hue, from the first scarlet splash of maple in the spruce woods in early October until the last fluttering leaves of the

poplars fall in late November, and the undergrowth of scarlet creeper on the purple rocks begins to mark the sombre decline of the year in December. The coming of snow gives evidence of the changing rhythm and order of colour. Keen air, blue and green skies, bright sunlight make a thousand baffling qualities of colour, in light and shadow, on the snow.

We spent one summer among the mountains. A number of fine sketches and canvases came out of that trip, but Lismer never went back. In later years he and my mother went regularly to British Columbia, but they passed rapidly through the mountains to stay on the west coast of Vancouver Island.

I believe that my mother's feeling for the mountains was the reason he never felt the desire to repeat this experience. Mother was usually adaptable to any situation. But I remember when we were in the mountains, at Lake O'Hara, she was upset at their closeness. She preferred the open shore and surf of the sea coast, or the high sky and low islands of Georgian Bay. My father would never have suggested that she go again to a place where she would be unhappy. His first concern would be for her.

The criterion for choosing a vacation spot seems to have been its remoteness. The place requiring the most complicated system of transportation won the toss. We generally set out in a comfortable train; then spent the night in a noisy hotel, in order to start out at dawn in another direction. This might also be by train, but one of a different vintage. It set us down at a whistle-stop where someone, we hoped, would be waiting for us with a boat. The last stage of the journey was usually by water. I can also remember, in the early twenties, several bumpy miles by horse and buggy. The trip home after the holiday was sometimes even more uncomfortable. Then we might start out before daylight in order to meet a train at that whistle-stop at seven in the morning — if it was on time.

There was one item that was less troublesome on the homeward journey. Less baggage! We always travelled with a small mountain of possessions. It did not matter whether we were rowing two miles up the coast or going round the world. When we went to an inaccessible spot in Georgian Bay we had an extra load, for then we needed food and bedding in addition to personal possessions and the painting gear. At every change to a new mode of transportation all the baggage had to be shifted. I cannot imagine how we got it into that horse-drawn buggy.

Mountain Climbing, B.C. 1928

Exit Lismers, 1928

Preparations for a month away from home were always formidable. In 1946 I had a letter from my father, written as he and Mother were preparing for a trip to Georgian Bay, staying this time in a hotel:

> The house looks tonight as it always looks before a trip. I have been ready for weeks, it seems — paint, panels, paper, and the usual number of suitcases and packets, which we don't seem to whittle down to less than eight pieces, with my own numbering five. At 61 I still seem to think I can do as much sketching as ever on a vacation; and I never wanted to get away as much before, and I never had so many ideas of doing new things in new ways. Whether I can do it or not is another matter.... Mother, dear soul, just goes along for the ride, but is as keen as ever to see that all transportation, boats and trains and other matters, is pre-arranged. She always gives me the impression that the railway and boat people just do things on a schedule written and ordained by your dear Mother.
>
> Anyway, we are going to enjoy a happy vacation together, and it wouldn't be if we had to go or stay separately.

Enclosed in the same letter was a three-part cartoon, anticipating the various joys of their coming vacation.

The lure of the Bay was not just good sketching. It was also an attractive way of life. We spent most of the day outdoors, independent of people and schedules. There was, however, a definite pattern to our days. My father often went for an early swim. After breakfast, which he frequently prepared, we hurried through the household chores. Mother packed a picnic basket and once more we loaded up the boat.

We set off in a direction that Dad considered was a likely one for good sketching. He was always on the lookout for subjects, remembering something seen the previous day, or even two years ago. We recognized the trees he had painted earlier. So often they had died in the interim — ruined by him, we would say. The truth was that the trees he chose to paint were already decrepit.

After mooring the boat we dragged ashore the basket, the books, Mother's knitting bag, the paints and the panels, not forgetting the coffee pot and the frying pan. In addition, there was our small Scotch Terrier barking her head off and wild to get ashore and start chasing the frogs. Dad wandered off, searching for a place to settle.

The Joys Ahead, 1946

Mother and I could always find a comfortable nook in which to sit and read and knit. Mother was a great knitter. Socks were her specialty and she was able to read and knit at the same time.

In about two hours, whenever he finished a sketch, Dad reappeared and made a camp fire. The meal varied according to our supplies — eggs, beans, bacon. Occasionally someone would give us a freshly caught fish, but my father was no fisherman. Even if we were having cold sandwiches he still made a fire and boiled water for coffee. It was not so much that he loved coffee, but that he enjoyed building a fire. When he drank coffee he liked two teaspoons of sugar in it. One awful day I forgot to pack any in the picnic basket. He substituted strawberry jam. No good! He added a couple of peppermint candies. Worse! He drew a cartoon as a memorial to the occasion.

No Sugar For the Coffee, Georgian Bay, 1931

If the weather remained clear after lunch, and there was another subject waiting, he made a second sketch. If the wind was rising, we headed for home. My father stoutly maintained that no matter in which direction he was rowing it was always against the wind. We have been in a few scary situations, with squalls too rough for a small boat. Dad had a strong rowing arm, however, and we never upset.

On the other hand, we frequently went aground in shallow water. He had the strongest desire to see over the next hill, round the next bend, or up some little stream. We attempted all sorts of channels on the chance they would lead to open water. If the going got tough, and he could not row or punt the boat, he took off his shoes, rolled up his trousers and towed us along. Many a time we got through to deeper water.

If we were back at the cottage early enough for an afternoon swim, we all went in the water, but with varying degrees of enthusiasm. I never really enjoyed the water. This annoyed my father because he thought I was not making the most of my opportunities. My mother had never learned to swim, so she had a quick dip and considered her duty was done. Dad was a fairly good swimmer and enjoyed the water. He could float around on his back, puffing at his beloved pipe.

In the evening, after dinner, we strolled around the island or took the boat and quietly rowed along the shoreline, looking at the reflections and watching the little animals that appeared at dusk. If the evening light interested him, Dad made another sketch. After dark we lighted the lamps and read or wrote until bedtime.

That was life in Georgian Bay when we lived in a rented cottage. In other places — the Maritimes, the Rockies, Quebec — we lived in hotels and boarding houses. There we encountered more people and there was a schedule for meals. But a similar pattern persisted; a sketch in the morning, maybe another after lunch (but more likely a nap), and a stroll along a country road in the evening.

Everywhere my father went in Canada he met people who knew him. They might have heard him lecture, or had been a student of his, or had a child in one of his Saturday morning classes. In later years he encountered men and women who had themselves been children in his classes. And so it went.

62

Georgian Bay Weather, 1931

Basutoland.

Three   South Wind

Most vacations were chosen on the basis of good painting sites. We did, however, spend several months, and on one occasion a whole year, in what were essentially working periods for my father.

There was a trip to England in the summer of 1924, the first time my parents had been back since they were married there in 1912. Most of the time was taken up with visits to relatives and friends. That was also the year of the first British Empire Exhibition at Wembly, which stirred up a lot of controversy in Canada over the many 'modern' paintings that had been chosen to represent Canada. These were well received in England and several pictures by members of the Group of Seven were given enthusiastic reviews. We went to see the exhibit a number of times while we were in London, and I am sorry to say that I remember nothing about it. On the other hand, I was much impressed by the Queen's Dolls' House which was displayed in the same building. I was then eleven years old, and at that time my father and I did not share all the same interests.

The next summer trip abroad was to Europe in 1932. This began at Nice, in the south of France, with the World Conference of the New Educational Fellowship, at which Lismer gave several lectures. From there we gathered up a small group and toured the galleries and churches of Rome, Florence, Venice, and then to Paris and London. The high spot of the trip, for my father, came through an introduction from Eric Brown of the National Gallery of Canada to a fellow curator at the Uffizi Gallery in Florence. Dad went off to present his credentials. He returned later with a bemused expression. He had held in his hands original drawings by Leonardo da Vinci.

Other long trips outside Canada introduced Lismer to a completely new environment, the Southern Dominions. In 1934 he was enchanted with South Africa — its people, its flowers, and the light on the distant hills. When he was invited to return for a year, in 1936, he was happy to go back.

This time he took his paints, although he left the bulky oils and panels behind and turned to water-colour. It was not a new medium for him, but one he rarely used. He found it well suited to the subtle colours of the South African scenery. A number of fine flower studies and landscapes were the result of this experience in a new environment.

But he did not neglect his pencil and paper. At each conference he attended, with characteristic wit he drew his fellow delegates. The caricatures appeared in the local press and the originals were snatched up by the victims and proudly displayed. Lismer identified himself, in a newspaper interview, as 'amuser-in-chief to the rest of the conference members'.

The year spent in South Africa was an exciting experience for Lismer. To his dismay he found he was regarded as an expert — and he had an expressed distrust of all so-called experts. As a newcomer, unacquainted with the problems of a strange country he was wary of telling his audiences how to run their affairs. To a group in Cape Town he said:

> I feel rather like a mariner who has put out to sea and having by good fortune landed upon the shores of a sister dominion — a strange land to a northerner from another land which holds part of its territory within the Arctic Circle. Here I find everything — the foliage and flowers, the birds, the colour of this marvelous panorama of coast scenery, all the strange and thrilling vistas — soothing and entrancing to one nine thousand miles away from home. Yet I feel like an intruder, willing to speak and yet afraid of injuring cherished conventions and still more established traditions.

> If I were speaking in the United States or in my own country, I would not be backward in telling the 'powers that be' where they are wrong, but here I am an ignorant educationist in art who apparently presumes to come to a new country, old in history, wise in the appreciation of her own difficult problems — and without understanding them, nor with any hope of fully grasping the difficulties your peculiar position presents — I attempt to tell **you** what I think about art and its presentation.

> It happens that I am not an orthodox educationist at all. I know so little about the rules and regulations, for I was not trained to respect the shining lights in the firmament of bureaus and departments, nor have I been drilled in the correct attitudes to curricula and textbooks. I must confess that my blind eye reads them only to see them as a means to an end — a sort of starting point, a jumping off place into the sea of experiment and adventure.

> Reading over many of the various systems of art education outlined in elementary and secondary education I cannot think that they were ever intended to be taken seriously, as being the only guide and final word in the teacher's life, to be

Zulu Warrior, 1934

slavishly followed — for fear some terrible ogre of an inspector ... should bring down the official axe heavily upon our dented and willing heads. I find that authority in education is quite willing to welcome independence where such independence achieves, but necessarily does not welcome idle and futile meanderings and useless experiment.

Lismer got along well with nearly everyone he met in South Africa, students and administrators alike. He made it clear that he, too, was learning. He was impressed with the earnestness of the students and their willingness to listen to a stranger. He lectured in a wide variety of places — in native villages, at Mission schools, to teachers and to children. He spoke in Art Galleries and Town Halls to large public audiences. On several occasions arrangements were less than perfect. The lantern often broke down, or was not available; the room was too cold or the acoustics poor. On at least two occasions all activity had to come to a halt while a violent hailstorm clattered on the tin roof.

Once, in Cape Town, Lismer walked out on one of his own lectures. He was invited to speak at a regular monthly meeting of a social club. When he and my mother arrived another speech was in progress. They sat down to listen, after telling their hosts that they must leave by 10:30 P.M., to be sure of transportation home. In spite of this when the first speech was over they went on to their musical programme. At 10:28 Mother and Dad slipped quietly away. I wish I knew what went on back at the club hall. As far as I know nothing further was ever said.

In his lectures to teachers during the educational conferences in South Africa, Australia, and New Zealand my father drew large and enthusiastic audiences. His methods might be unorthodox, but his approach was successful. His audience never knew quite what to expect. After his first lecture in any series it was always necessary to provide a larger hall for the next one. One reporter in Melbourne, Australia, wrote: "Things ran pleasantly off-schedule when Mr. A. Lismer, the genial philosopher in charge of art education at the Toronto Art Gallery, addressed the New Educational Fellowship in the big lecture theatre at the University today. He announced cheerfully that he had not the slightest intention of talking on the subject set for him."

73

He was sensitive to the mood or the nature of an audience. He entered into good-humoured banter with sober businessmen. Elderly ladies were charmed into delighted laughter. With children he was at his best, teasing and encouraging until every child was responding. None of these actions was forced or artificial. He fell into a natural rapport with each group.

Arthur Lismer was really a great showman. He knew how to stage a performance. He could present a lecture, a picture, or a class project in such a way that he held his audience while they slowly and painlessly absorbed his message.

An early story demonstrated this touch of the dramatic that did not, however, go according to plan. In his student days in Sheffield, Lismer belonged to a sketching club that had a favorite meeting place at a pub on the moors outside the city. Near *The Three Merry Lads* my father made a speech in which he pretended he had a box of a magic potion to cure all ills. He spoke so eloquently that a crowd gathered and soon demanded that he open the box (which was really his sketch box) and begin selling the contents. In the end my father's friends had to hustle him into the pub before the angry crowd got out of hand.

While he was still in Sheffield Lismer performed with the Sheffield School of Art Musical and Dramatic Club. This interest in the theatre stayed with him all his life. In Toronto in the early twenties he designed stage sets and costumes at Hart House Theatre in the University of Toronto. About the same time he designed stage settings for French Canadian and for English folk-song festivals in Quebec City, Toronto, and Banff. Later, when he worked with children at the Art Gallery of Toronto (now the Art Gallery of Ontario) and the Montreal Museum of Fine Arts he produced spectacular pageants every year, for which the children designed the sets and costumes. Lismer directed the action and often wrote the script.

On more informal occasions he could enliven a group with his wit, imitations, quick sketches, and simple sleight-of-hand tricks. He was great at charades and loved dressing up, creating an illusion out of almost nothing. His flair for the dramatic was also evident when he told a story, and especially so when he was being pressed for information about himself. He could say the most outrageous things with a straight face. Possibly his remarks might appear in print. I expect some reporters who had never met him before did not know whether to believe him or not.

Lions Sleeping, 1936

I have heard him add details to a story each time he repeated it, embroidering the basic facts to make the tale worth telling. Occasionally, I would protest and remind him that he was not recalling the event correctly. This made very little impression on him. Mother, on the other hand, could bring him up short with the facts. When we were on a lengthy trip she kept a diary in which she recorded dates, names, and places. She was able to point out what really happened and Dad would not argue. But I doubt if he remembered for long.

In my younger days this enthusiastic showmanship caused me occasional embarrassment. I was over-sensitive about anything that appeared different from the crowd. Other girls' fathers did not draw pictures on menus and table mats in a restaurant. They did not do funny tricks and imitations at children's parties. Those fathers were generally very dignified and no one laughed. I grew out of that feeling, however, and could enjoy him as he was. His enthusiasm was catching and it was obvious that people listened to what he had to say.

This ability to communicate his enthusiasm to others was strong. He saw deeply into common things and he wanted others to perceive these depths. He opened wide a wonderful world to those who chose to follow. For the children he was a sort of Pied Piper, leading them on to new adventures, directing their eyes to hidden things, and their curiosity to new discoveries. To the adults, those who had grown beyond a child's imagination, he suggested that they still had talents that could enrich their lives. Appreciation was an art in which all could share. It was the key to understanding and participation in the artistic process. But he repeated again and again that appreciation was not just **reception** but **response.** This response he defined as 'the capacity to take steps forward into new vistas and deeper into one's own nature'.

But we have wandered away from South Africa. We should get back to that lovely place. People were pleasant and hospitable everywhere. While my father was working, if Mother and I were around, they made sure we were entertained with morning tea and drives through the countryside. It was a strenuous life because friends, in their kindness, tried to fill every moment. It seemed that we were always being taken to the top of something in order to admire the vista — great expanses of scenery stretching away to the horizon. We also visited lovely gardens and fine zoos.

We were taken to see native villages, Bushman rock paintings, beautiful old Dutch buildings, and to meet so many interesting people. Then the whole routine was repeated in Australia and again in New Zealand, each country unique and presenting new experiences.

The whole year in South Africa was one great adventure. It was at times tiring, frustrating, but infinitely rewarding. My father saw a good deal more of the country than Mother and I did. He would be off for a week or so at a time, giving short courses to teachers in remote training centres. For the first six months our home base was an apartment in Johannesburg. Then we moved south to Cape Town to a guest house high on a hillside overlooking False Bay. We were there about four months and then left for Durban on the East Coast. In May, 1937, we sailed from there to Australia.

Australia and New Zealand were equally fascinating, but our stay there was much shorter, about three months. On our way home across the Pacific our ship stopped at Suva in the Fiji Islands, for about twelve crowded hours. I think we filled every one of them. My father gave a lecture in the Town Hall, and Mother and I went shopping along the docks. We all visited a boys' school up in the hills and were entertained with a concert of singing and dancing by the students. We were then taken for an extensive drive to see the sights of Suva. We called upon two local artists and Dad was asked to criticize their work — which was unfair to both sides on a first meeting. We were taken to a cocktail party which was celebrating an engagement. After insisting that we wanted to go back to the ship for dinner we were allowed to do so. But after dinner a group of people showed up to spend the evening. It was all very pleasant, but hectic. The ship sailed at midnight. The next day we crossed the International Date Line and we had the day all over again, but this time it was much more relaxing.

It was with great excitement and real joy that we approached Canada. We had been gone sixteen months in all and were very happy to be home again.

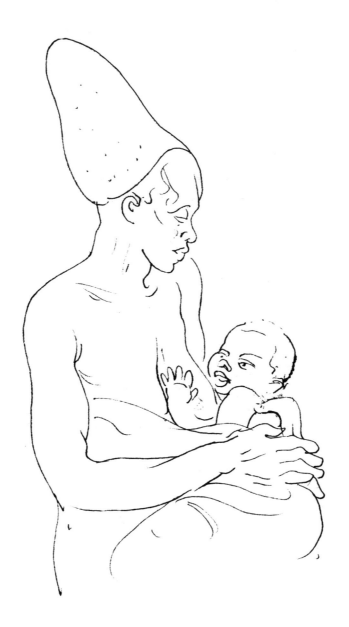

African Mother, 1936

Four   Two Rocks in a Pool

Lismer's normal winter-time schedule was crowded and demanding. He seldom refused a request for help or advice, was always able to fit in one more activity. But when the chance came for him to relax he had many ways of unwinding. He could take a quick nap, fall asleep at once, and awake refreshed in an hour. He read detective stories, worked complicated crossword puzzles, and enjoyed a good movie. In spite of his many evening lectures he and Mother went to plays and concerts. On rare occasions he was even inveigled into attending an affair at my school.

He called himself a Sunday painter, which implied a hobby rather than a vocation. However they were classified, painting and drawing were his most satisfying forms of relaxation. They were also the expression of his deep conviction that creative activity was necessary for survival. He wrote in 1946:

> No road is too long, no experience is without creative interest, no vocation or leisure hour is empty of meaning, for the person who has within himself vision and some skill to occupy himself with some creative act — whether it is painting a landscape, modelling in clay, writing a poem, or thinking about problems of housing and how other people live.... Art is like this — it is experience lived and shared with others. It is the living sinew that binds humans together everywhere; for no nation, no child, no person is without it. It is the part of our nature that responds to sights and sounds of beauty. All education should be saturated with a liberal infusion of the natural instinct of man to create. Artist-minded people and artists who do things in any medium are the ones that can do this for others.

When Lismer was not drawing he seems to have been writing. He left thousands upon thousands of words. He wrote sensitive and lyrical prose, building pictures with words as he did with paint. From this it was only a step into poetry.

Doggerel verse came easily, tossed off to suit an occasion and seldom recorded. A few have survived. One such poem was directed at two of his friends who were becoming more and more abstract in their painting:

> *Ye Brooker and ye Harris, now listen all to me.*
> *Ye may have been to Paris, but ye canna draw a tree.*
> *These stunted apparitions with wildly waving arms*
> *Are merely suppositions that give the public qualms.*
> *But take some consolation from the poet who wrote for thee,*
> *In the scheme of all creation, 'Only God can make a tree'.*

The more formal verse came less easily and less frequently. At any rate, very few are extant. The few scraps that have survived reveal false starts and much revision. I find his thoughts obscured at times, but a deep feeling comes through.

> *I stand at the parting place of pathways broad;*
> *At the edge of vision wide*
> *My spirit dares to venture into realms untrod,*
> *Moved by relentless tide*
> *Onward and upward, forward and down,*
> *Touching the crests of thought;*
> *Glimpsing the gleam of the far-off crown*
> *By countless ages wrought.*
> *Old thoughts, old doubts, ideals worn,*
> *False pride, ill will, and wasteful creed*
> *Uproot themselves, all thin and torn*
> *Leave ready earth for fruitful seed.*

Several members of the Group of Seven wrote poetry. Both Lawren Harris and J.E.H. MacDonald published their verse. I do not think that Lismer revealed his more serious efforts at poetic composition. At least, I was unaware of them. None was published and he left very little upon which to judge his efforts. His more informal verses were better known, and were used to entertain his family and his friends.

Lismer's reading was wide and varied. Notes made for lectures reveal the many authors that he consulted — philosophers, educationists, art historians, and biographers of creative men. On at least one occasion he gave a lecture on "Art and Literature". There is apparently no copy of the text of this lecture, but the preliminary research for it shows that he was collecting quotations from the English lyrical poets, those who had a pictorial quality in their verse and a deep appreciation of nature. In addition, my father had a strong affinity for the American poet, Walt Whitman, and quoted him frequently.

There is one poem that I found among his papers that puzzles me. It seems familiar, yet I cannot find the author. I have searched diligently and have asked for help from several people. The name escapes us all. Lismer thought enough of the

LLD from McGill, 1863

ME

THE
MEDAL!

Honours, 1963 and The Medal, 1967

· THE GROUP OF SEVEN

1952

The New Group — Janet, Grandpa, Barby, Grandma, Phil, Carol, Marjorie, 1952

Roast Pig at Luau, Hawaii, 1938

poem to write it down in full. He quoted the last two lines in a lecture and also in a magazine article. In the latter he preceded the quotation with "in the words of the ancient Chinese poet", but even this clue proved fruitless. Of course, my father might very easily have said that, in order to cover up the fact that he also did not know its source.

The poem, whoever wrote it, is worth quoting, since Lismer chose to record it, and it so well expresses his philosophy of art. It is called *The Painter's Precept:*

I would not paint a face
Or rocks, or streams, or trees,
Mere semblance of things
But something more than these.

I would not play a tune
Upon the string or lute
Which did not also sing
Meanings that else were mute.

That art is best which gives
To the soul's range no bound
Something beside the form
Something beyond the sound.

For relaxation my father enjoyed detective stories, generally those of the milder English school. He was not a violent man and did not look for violence in his entertainment. When it came to the reading of 'good' literature both my father and I left that to Mother. She enjoyed well written books of fiction and travel. In later years, she also read mystery and detective stories, most of them by English women writers. But my father had no use at all for those.

When he had leisure time, my father preferred to spend it outdoors. On vacations this was easy. While at home he relied on gardening and walking. In a letter written from the depths of New York City, in 1938, he expressed his longing for open spaces and things that grew. There, and in any city in which they found themselves, my parents spent much time in the public gardens and zoological parks as an antidote to the crowded streets.

The first garden that I can remember belonged to J.E.H. MacDonald in Thornhill — the famous tangled garden. For several months in 1915 we lived with the Mac-Donalds and my father helped in the garden. When we moved to our small house, not far away, he grew his own flowers and vegetables. He illustrated these in several sketches and at least one canvas. In Bedford, Nova Scotia, during the war years our garden was a source of fresh produce for the summer and canned goods for the rest of the year. The soil was rich and very productive. My father often recalled that garden, and those vegetables grew bigger and bigger — like the fish that got away.

We bought a house in Toronto in the fall of 1919, the only property that my father ever owned. With the house we acquired a plot of weeds, a tangle of current bushes, an apple tree, and, temporarily, a chicken house with twelve chickens. By the next spring, the chickens had been reclaimed by their owner, and Dad went to work clearing the weeds and planting vegetables in the back garden. The following year, he bought the lot next door and built a studio at the rear. He planned, and planted, a wide perennial border down one side and across the street front. It was full of lovely flowers and prize shrubs. We had a gardener for a little while, but he kept pulling up the plants my father had just put in. We discovered the man was half blind and operated on the principal that all small plants were weeds. In later years Dad lacked the time for extensive gardening. But even a short time outdoors was relaxing.

96

Esther and the Dog, 1920

After my parents moved to Montreal they lived in a pleasant apartment overlooking a lovely garden. They enjoyed it, but they had no part in it. Dad missed a piece of ground to call his own. Whenever he visited us in Maryland he spoke wistfully of having a garden again. He never did. It was one of the regrets of his later life.

Walking was both for adventure and relaxation. It was a great experience, especially for a child, to walk along a country road with my father. Our three daughters always looked forward to their grandparents' annual visit. On a walk with Grandpa they saw their own neighborhood from a different point of view. He talked about the clouds and the trees. He drew pictures in the dust or fashioned an animal from wet clay by the roadside. A stone, picked up along the way, was never just a gray lump. It was smooth to the touch; it had a pleasing shape; smeared with a wet finger, it revealed unexpected colours. Two dots added with a pencil turned it into a monster or a mouse. For a child, that stone became a treasure.

At the seashore it was not the grand vistas of waves and sky that held his interest. It was the rocky pools left by the tide, with rounded pebbles and sea-worn shells. In Georgian Bay the little puddles and backwaters with darting fish and lilypads fascinated him. He painted a canvas of one of these, *Two Rocks in a Pool,* which my mother liked so well she would not let him sell it. It is still in our home.

My father's pockets, after a country walk, were always full. There would be colourful stones, a pine-cone twisted into a pattern, a broken snail shell with the convolutions revealed, or a few autumn leaves of vivid hue. He invariably collected a tiny bouquet of wild flowers and grasses, which he then presented to Mother, to pin on her coat or dress. The last time they visited us, in 1968, he was still bringing this little tribute from outdoors and she was still gracefully accepting it.

No account of the life of Arthur Lismer is complete without an understanding of the role of his wife, Esther. On the title page of her copy of the catalogue for Lismer's Retrospective Show in 1950 he wrote: ''This whole exhibition and all the paintings in it — and all the honours — shared and experienced by Esther with the guy who painted them.'' This was a sincere and deeply felt tribute to her place in his life.

My mother was the sister of one of my father's close friends in Sheffield, a fellow artist and sketching companion. She visited her brother from time to time, met Arthur, and they became engaged in the fall of 1908. It was four years before he was earning enough to enable them to marry. He was then in Toronto, but returned to England in 1912 and brought her back to Canada.

She was with Arthur on his first trip to Georgian Bay in September 1913. I do not think that either of them knew what to expect, but it was a happy and exciting adventure. In later years my mother wondered how she had had the temerity to take a four-month-old baby into the unknown. But we all survived. Esther adapted quickly wherever she was, and was always ready for a new experience. She enjoyed all forms of travel and handled the logistics of our trips. Her ability to read a timetable intelligently never ceased to amaze my father.

She used to say that she had 'no accomplishments', meaning by that no professional skills. But she had a high degree of all the domestic skills and, in addition, she was an excellent business manager. We needed one in the family, and it certainly was not my father. Her greatest accomplishment, however, was her capacity for making a home. She provided the haven that my father needed, a place of serenity where he could renew his energies. She was there with sympathy and encouragement. She might not say very much, but she would always listen.

Not only did she provide a quiet and serene retreat, but she acted as a buffer between Arthur's disinclination to say 'no', and those who would take advantage of this. He was constantly being asked to attend meetings, give talks, or write articles. Mother did not interfere, but she made it difficult for people to reach him when he was at home. There was a time when he was overwhelmed with phone calls at dinner time. It reached a point where he scarcely ever ate a hot meal. Then my mother put her foot down and decreed that either she or I would answer all calls and take messages.

People with an effusive or pretentious manner annoyed my mother and embarrassed my father, even if their sincerity was not in question. Dad could handle such manners with a quip. But she did not have that defence and became cool and polite. In talking it over later it would seem amusing and the incident would be forgotten — unless my father drew a cartoon about it.

MOTHER LOOKS UP THE NEXT TRAIN

The Next Train, Cape Breton Island, 1940

It Was a Lovely Talk, 1932

I remember one occasion when we were all acutely uncomfortable. After one of my father's lectures, in South Africa, the chairman rose to thank the speaker. He announced that we would all pay tribute to this great man by standing for a minute of silent recognition. Mother and I stood up also, feeling very silly. I have no idea how my father looked, for I dared not even glance at him. To catch his eye at that moment would have been a disaster. "I felt such a darn fool," he said later.

Mother did not care to look ridiculous either. When a radio script was submitted to Dad for his approval (since it concerned his biography) she also had something to say about it. The writer had taken off on a flight of fancy that irritated her. The script indicated that Arthur and Esther were watching the wind and the waves on Georgian Bay:

<u>Wife</u> — I love that pine tree over there — the big one standing up so sturdily against the wind.

<u>Lismer</u> — There's a wonderful pattern and design here. Look at the way the waves sweep across — the clouds march in the sky with them.

<u>Wife</u> — (TRIUMPHANTLY) You're planning a picture. You're planning a picture. I know you are.

<u>Lismer</u> — Maybe.

<u>Wife</u> — I can always tell by that gleam in your eye. Isn't it wonderful, planning a picture in a September gale?

My father wrote in the margin of the script: "My wife thinks this is just goofy." He then reduced the last three speeches to one remark by my mother: "You'd better paint it, if you feel that way." This was much closer to something she might have said.

She had a practical response to most situations. Within the family she expressed her opinions freely, but was rather quiet when she was with a group. Although I cannot recall an instance, I feel that she had a sobering affect upon Arthur's soaring idealism, and her good sense could return him once more to reality.

For his part, my father considered her wishes and her welfare on all occasions. There were, of course, differences of opinion, shared disappointments, and difficult decisions to make. There was also much laughter and joy and a high sense of adventure. For fifty-seven years they knew these things together.

Dancing Woman (undated)

Five   Sunlight in a Wood

"The reason we are interested in art is because the subject matter is life. Any great work of art, for this reason alone, has a universality in its appeal. It is the only language that all nations and peoples **use** and understand. It is the ultimate unifying element in a world divided against itself."

This was Lismer's basic approach to the meaning of art. Time and again he confirmed this universality of art, at least to his own satisfaction, as he travelled through other communities and into different cultures. He insisted that we must all become participators in the experience of **living** art, not appear as mere onlookers.

To do this we must develop the art of appreciation; which simply meant seeing the world with the eyes of artists. "If the artist is within ourselves, so much the better." Appreciation from a responsive audience is important to the creative artist. All of us have experiences that, suddenly, we wish to share with someone — a wave dashing on the rocks, a view from a hilltop, or a snatch of music. Lismer saw this trait in man as another aspect of the universality of art and he wrote:

> Something happens and life is changed ever so little, but it is there, a new and wonderful experience. Now, the artist does something about these things; writes a novel or paints a picture; he composes a stanza of verse, or perhaps he just shares his wonder and pleasure with another and says, 'It's a great day.' That's the creative spirit in action and such things bind men together more than any other thing in life. We share.

Lismer knew that children had this sense of wonder and a desire to share, and that these could be lost in adolescence. Moreover, many adults believed that the surprise and excitement about the wonders of the world were over, and that there was no more magic:

> Don't you believe it. Inside each one of us is an artist. In fact in children this imaginative quality is strong and vital, but we think always that some other person, not ourself, has this quality and we will have to grind along at some dull routine job absorbing facts and histories and never see the world or make a picture or design a house. Let me tell you this, and I know it is true. If you would truly live and see the world, commence right now in your own city, village or anywhere in your home and school, to put down what you see. VISUALIZE life.

Make a picture of it, the people, the houses and farms, the woods and animals, the birds and flowers. Find out why they are there and why you are there, explore the countryside and the history, the folk-tales, the songs and the patterns of things about you — but DRAW it — not words, but lines, colours and designs. In time, and it is not a long time either, your curiosity will take you further afield and your horizons will have widened and you will want to know more about what is on the other side of almost everything. History, geography, nature study, biology, science all come alive after a while — they are not subjects in your school programme only, they are touched with magic, romance, adventure — they have the quality that we call art.

And that's what an artist is, a child who has never lost the gift of looking at life with curiosity and wonder. Art is not the exclusive possession of those who can draw, write poems, make music, or design buildings. It belongs to all those who can see their way through all things with imagination.

Have your dreams, build your castles, travel to far countries on the wings of thought — but you can only make them come true if you exercise the wish to share them with others — to put them down — to see them clearly. And that's another thing an artist can do — he can see further and deeper than others and he never keeps it to himself. He lets others share it.

He invites us to enjoy and to listen, to look and to contemplate. From this we learn to see our own world as we never saw it before.... Even if we ourselves cannot travel far and wide, a world of wonder about simple things of beauty and imagination opens out slowly before us, and life becomes richer and brighter. We can do our work of giving service to others because we, too, have caught the gleam — we can see — we are all artists.

He might have added, "or artist-minded people", a phrase he often used when he referred to those who were not necessarily poets, or painters, or musicians. These were the individuals who thought creatively and had a lively curiosity about the world:

These people have the clue to a deeper reality.... The creative thinking and doing of such individuals is the sustaining factor that keeps the spirit sane in a world rocked with possessive creeds and actions.

110

Shipyard, Gaspé, 1927

According to Lismer, those who did not have this quality of curiosity and excitement led second-hand lives. They existed through the thoughts of others. Entertainment by radio, television, movies, and gossip columns was never an adequate substitute for first-hand participation in creative living. It was the **exclusive** reliance upon this type of entertainment to which he referred, for he enjoyed all these things — not, however, to the exclusion of other activities.

He believed it was the moral obligation of every individual to respond to his environment with sensitivity and sound judgement. Eventually, it was hoped, imaginative people would be able to banish the banal and the vulgar. Above all, apathy would disappear, driven away by those who challenged it. It was man's indifference to his surroundings that Lismer considered the greatest foe. He fought it constantly on every front.

This strong desire to make people aware of the deficiencies of their environment sometimes led him into trouble. He was apt to make sweeping statements that were picked up by the press and made into headlines. His remarks were, perhaps, reported out of context or the meaning missed. A controversy would start. There would be letters to the local papers and protests from civic leaders. Even the National Gallery was once drawn into a dispute and requested Lismer to explain what was going on.

On one occasion the Art Gallery of Toronto inquired if Lismer had been misquoted in a Montreal speech, in which he had been reported as saying that Canadian businessmen were the dullest in creation and the loudest in their accusations against art. Since two newspapers quoted him in identical words I expect he did say it; and he probably meant it at the time. He certainly set a good many people thinking — including the businessmen, many of whom are, today, strongly supportive of the arts.

He attacked the lack of feeling for beauty in various places that he visited. Naturally, this received mixed support from the citizens. In Johannesburg, South Africa, he objected to the dumps from the gold mines that surrounded the city. But many people cherished these and resented his criticism. On a later visit he saw those long, pale, flattened hills in a different light (in both senses of the word) and was willing to acknowledge their appeal.

In Toronto he deplored the shoddy buildings and ugly advertising signs along Yonge Street. He saw these every day on his streetcar ride into town. He found the whole aspect of the street unattractive. A few years later, in Montreal, he said much the same about St. Catherine Street. In both cities, however, there were many people who agreed with him.

Perhaps many such remarks were spontaneous. But I am sure that others were calculated attempts to stir up a 'divine discontent', as he once put it, with anything within the experience of his audience that was ugly or banal:

> We cannot look around our cities today and see without pain all the ugliness that man has created to express his possessiveness. The ugly rows of houses, the mean little shops, the brutally stark factories and sordid railway sidings, compare these with a little gothic town or an English village and feel the difference and the price we have paid when science and industry, and not art, have created standards of living. Until we see that beauty and art are absolute necessities of living, we shall not escape from those masters of our destinies who plan only for a temporary world of power and possessiveness, and not for a future where beauty can live more commonly in the hearts of men.
>
> There is a way out that is worth trying, even if our present adult population is past praying for. It is possible still with the younger generation of youth and with young children to form intelligent ways of developing habits of thoughtful and enjoyable experience, with art as the crown of life, instead of the footstool.... Give the child art in his most rhythmic and vital period of growth and we feed him with the means to keep his senses keen and the spirit alert. It does not matter whether he becomes an artist or not, that is another question, but it does matter whether he adopts too early a merely predacious attitude to his fellowmen, or whether he sees creatively and with understanding and recognition the various stepping stones to higher things that he will encounter on his own particular highway. Encourage the understanding of contemporary art, which includes all endeavours to create civic beauty. Give him the capacity to enjoy the experience of 'five senses tingling with delight', and destroy the puritanical hostility to art and beauty that seems to be the natural state of the adult mind.

Killocks and Floats, 1946

116

Ontario Barns, 1927

Anonymous, 1932

Lismer wanted an ideal world, full of peace and beauty, in which the communities would be harmonious, and the people busy with creative work. There would be no idle hands to lead to mischief. It was a dream many men have had in the past, and will continue to hope for the future. If people were different, with greater concern for their fellows, it might be achieved. He acknowledged this to be idealism. He recognized that the artist was a visionary and a dreamer, the natural leader of idealistic thought, since the creative person readily responded to beauty and order in life. But the apathy that he encountered could be deadly.

My father had a practical side. He knew that men were not as cooperative as they might be; were slow to accept ideas they did not understand, and those for which they saw no purpose. He could see things as they were but this did not keep him from the battle. A good fight could arouse people enough to show that there were still signs of life. Response, any response, was better than indifference:

Art has always been atomic. It has bombarded the Philistines... at all vulnerable points, using every aesthetic weapon known to humans to pierce the veil of indifference and apathy.

There is Van Gogh pushing across the path and thrusting into the jungle — slashing and tearing his way through to emerge torn and bleeding, mad and frustrated but with what treasures of vision, unseen by the careful ones. Or Rouault, Goya, Matisse, even Picasso all follow trails — or rather they cut paths of their own. All have breathed deeply of life, of new sights and visions of significance. All have brought new gifts, promise of new days to dawn from the promised land newly surveyed.

I expect he upset many people, hurt some feelings and even offended a few friends. It probably distressed him, on occasion. But it would not change his mind. He was firm in the belief that if all men worked together, as a democratic community, life could have beauty and purpose:

Somewhere within the artist is a divine unrest unsatisfied by the obvious sights and sounds of beauty. Conscious all the time that hidden things contain secrets, forms strange and full of energy, significance — colour intense, emotional, lyrical — moods and deep sentiments hardly of the visible world — meanings that have no visible source come in more or less vibrant and continuous fashion to every artist. The question of quality, of high value and penetration is whether he can deal with them visually, whether he can discard the obvious, the plain view — the imitative and trite — or whether seeing deeper and further than others — which is the mark of the supreme artist — he can pierce the veil of material objective things and arrive at the sentient core where design, form, colour, mystery, enchantment, and deep brooding secrets lie. The proof and the creative fulfilment is his capacity to achieve a new way, a more significant vision, a deeper insight into the meaning of life.

122

Children at Work (undated)

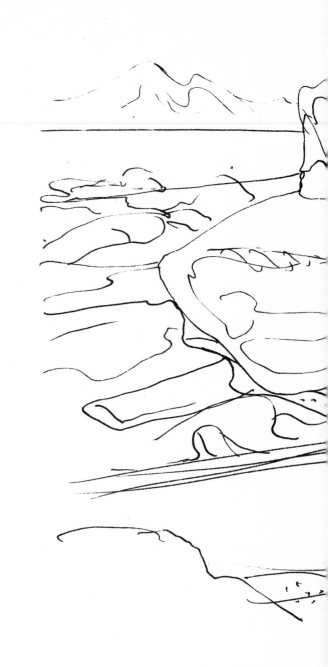

7·14·52

Six   The Canadian Jungle

When Arthur Lismer wrote or lectured on contemporary Canadian Art he was diffident about his own role, and generally managed to avoid personal references. He spoke with enthusiasm about the Group as a unit, and referred only occasionally to individual members — himself least of all. In an outline for a book on Canadian painting, that was never published, he wrote:

> I don't know where I personally appear in the book. I was in it up to my neck, but I think I can preserve the balance between interested spectator and participator, without offence and intrusion. I have no regrets that the Group of Seven is now 'old hat', and I have a lively interest and admiration for what is being attempted today.

It was this detachment that he maintained in later years. As the turbulent days of the Group receded, he spoke of them less and less. In the early years he had been eager to state the case for this new approach to the Canadian landscape. In a lecture in 1926 he said:

> Is it any wonder that with the newly opened opportunities to explore this background that the Canadian painter intuitively sensed a way out of the manifest ennui of decadent academicism of European art into an independence of thought and freedom from mere technical dexterity — that comes as a blight at times in the annals of the art of all nations. What a vast array of subject matter never before attempted by painters! And, incidentally, it was not the way these things were painted that gave objection, but that the painters were experimenting with forbidden forms — by which I mean not commonly accepted forms, not classical, not romantic. It was the stark realism of some aspect of the north country in its austerity and severe aloofness that appalled by its searching and objective reality. But consider what was happening. Commonplace picturesqueness disappears in the north country and is replaced by epical and powerfully moving shapes. Conventional paintings, easy atmospheric effects, tepid and noncommittal attack have, perforce, to be discarded. Here are noble shapes, strangely moving dramas of form and colour, effects of light and weather that make the timid one duck for shelter and send the bolder one farther afield. The north country is not by any means a timid painter's paradise. Gradually it was born in on these painters of a newer school... that there had to be a firm grasping

of the design and rhythm of mountain and stream, of the serrated aspect of spruce and pine against skies of such glorious clarity, unsurpassed in beauty in any other country in the world.

It was a new paradise, and a new idiom was needed, and if credit can be given to the Group of Seven, then it is that they moved the art of landscape painting into a more rhythmic and plastic idiom, more in harmony with the energy and quality of our national character.

By 1950, in a radio talk on Canadian Art, he saw the Group's activity in a different perspective, as,

… only one chapter in the total story of growth and development of art in this country …. We owed a great deal to each other, and to the warm contacts of friendship, and to a common theme — to paint Canada as we saw it, as we felt it, and according to our limited stature as well as we could. There was nothing technical in the revolt. We were never consciously rebellious — we attacked nothing but the landscape. The Group of Seven fought it out on the spot. They fought back at the pine trees and the rocks, the colour and design, and slogged out the problems of interpretations in all seasons and weathers.

Yes, it was crude and there was a lot of bad painting — but it was the first sign of free experiment in painting, independent of school, academy or weary conventions. The sterner discipline came later, and an art form born of enthusiasm and intelligent handling of material was created and turned into the quality, grandeur, austerity and simplicity of the Canadian scene…. Today these (paintings) appear mellow and simple, their sombreness accentuated — a little old-masterish, even romantic, and — in view of the later expressionism, irrationalism, surrealism, and automation of the avant-garde of 1950 — they appear even a little academic.

The friendship among these artists was deep and sustaining. Nevertheless, specific references are scarce in Lismer's written material. It seemed as if the same reserve that he applied to his own painting was extended to those closely associated with him. His articles about Varley, and Jackson, and the memorial for MacDonald were factual and rather impersonal. There must have been many informal occasions when my father talked freely with mutual friends, but of these times no record exists among his personal papers.

Georgian Bay, 1929

There was one memorable evening, however, that is on record. A dinner was given, in January 1942, for A.Y. Jackson when he received an honorary degree from Queen's University. Over two hundred of his friends were present and Arthur Lismer gave an informal address. It was a very friendly gathering and Lismer's style was suited to the occasion. He spoke warmly of Jackson and his contribution to Canadian culture. Early in his talk he told of Jackson's effect upon his own approach to the Canadian scene. In 1911 Jackson had exhibited his canvas, *The Edge of the Maple Wood,* at the annual show of the Ontario Society of Artists:

> I was a newcomer, raw English, full of enthusiasm for new scenes, but finding Canadians just a little strange and lacking in imagination, humour, and refinement. I **was** raw. I confess it. But I **knew** what this country was like. I had been in it at least two months! Then I saw this Jackson canvas.... I did not know a single Canadian work, except MacDonald's and then Jackson's. These raised my spirit and changed my views.... Jackson's *Maple Wood* created a feeling of settlement and permanency about a land of which my first impressions were impermanent and transient.

Later in the same speech Lismer remarked that it was impossible to separate Jackson from his friends; then he went on to speak of several of those who were closely associated with him:

> Thomson was the voyager, the discoverer; a little pop-eyed with wonder, mixed with surprise and awe, that colours and brushes in his grasp could give, even in so brief a manner, some quality of the nature he saw.... Thomson saw visions and dreams. His paintings were his visions made articulate. He was not a primitive. He was an intuitive mystic. He felt nature — he adored her — crept into her moods, ... and his canvases lived in the Canadian mind.
>
> MacDonald was a poet, also a dreamer, and a fine craftsman, equally at home with heraldry, a page of fine lettering, a nature poem or a verse in a tender mood. He loved old and mellow things, found epics in graveyards and warmth in old missals. His mysticism was deep and conscious.... He scorned badness in design and character. His art had a hedonistic quality. His sympathies were valiantly on the side of lowly souls and lofty things, but not on the side of virtuosity or the banal.... He fits into the Canadian picture, leads the choir and reads the text.

Harris is the man of dynamic action. He has ideas for everything and finds their solution in argument and cosmic speculation. He believes in the **illusion** of earth, the unreality of existence, and the permanence of change. His blue-print for life is continually undergoing change — change of heart, change of mind and action — but always with a purpose, to find a sort of perfection in living to prepare for a supreme perfection in a life beyond the senses and bodily existence. So **his** trees and houses, lakes and clouds are part of an ordered unfolding plan — incomplete, imperfect — but creating endlessly new forms. He moves with them and sees, in a big and noble manner, their relation to idea and creative purpose. It is inevitable that he should symbolize rather than represent. His abstractions represent exquisite balance and movement — cosmic, slow, and spacious. In the Canadian picture he is the beam of light in the infinity of space. He appeals to our sense of need for spiritual breathing space.

But Jackson, in this absurd grouping of characters, is definitely the painter, the explorer without humbug or superficial mysticism.... He represents a Rabelasian rotundity to MacDonald's gothic leanness — and he wears his halo cock-eyed.... His feet are solidly planted on the earth he loves; and his trees, his fences, and his houses belong to human beings who planted them solely for A.Y. to paint.

Weary Woman (undated)

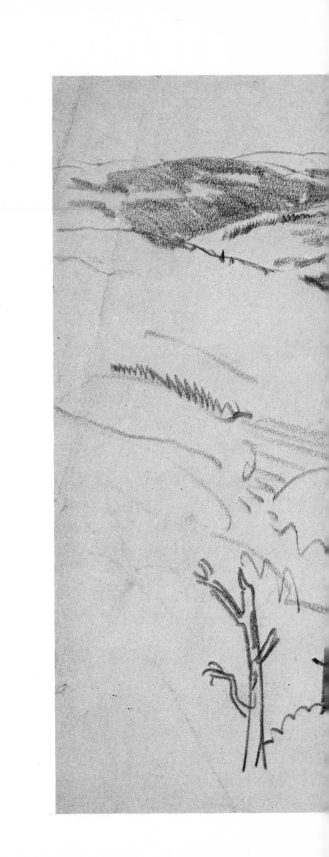

Seven   Storm Passing

From time to time someone has commented upon the so-called 'conflict' in Arthur Lismer's life; that he was obliged to give up a career as a painter in order to devote his time to teaching. The implication was always that this was a hardship for him and that he had been forced into a difficult choice. But my father saw no conflict between his activities as painter and teacher. The one enhanced the other, as he once explained:

> An artist needs and seeks many experiences to aid in his work and in his interest in, and service to, humanity in general. Teaching, or any other educational work I have attempted, is never a sideline. It is always part of a full life, and not an interlude between periods of studio activity. Art and education are both parts of the process of living and never separate. If I had done one, or either, I should have been better at that particular one than I am, but the constant pull at my natural ambitions as a painter and my interest in education has always been a life problem. The fact that I have done both is the peculair part of my curiosity about human beings — especially children — and of my early training as an artist.
>
> All artists should teach, or in some way help others to see, encourage them to create — if only on the assumption that life is much richer for all people if they can see further and deeper than others into the meaning and beauty of life. The reward over a matter of years is in seeing young people respond to their newly found sense of freedom and in the development of personality and richness of character which is the result of their growing curiosity about the nature and design of the world in which they live.

Lismer did not talk much about his own paintings. Asked directly, he was likely to turn the discussion into other channels. In 1956, however, after the showing of a film about the work with children at the Montreal Children's Art Centre, the script of the local television program called for a candid answer about his own work. For this he wrote the script himself:

> You'll know what happened in Toronto in the early days of the Group of Seven. It is old history, and to many, very old hat, but it sparked something. In my case, it is a collection of experiences and paintings in wide and rugged places that still breathe a sort of magic. But I think the vista, the expanse, and the sense of topography in light and colour have come to a focus — a more immediate foreground of things like the fishing gear at Cape Breton, and the lushness and

austerity of a forest — and even deeper and further into smaller forms of nature — shells, leaves, coral, anything organic. Even in such minute forms there is a vastness. There are vistas and design unsurpassed, at least to my myopic eyes. Nature need not be a standard, but it is a wonderful source of refreshment and delight.

I am excited about all modern trends. In Montreal there is a mingling of the racial origins of two great peoples. Canada owes much to the vivid natural exuberance and approach to the abstract of the French-Canadian artist, and this, integrated with the graphic realism of the English character in action, may yet place Canada high in art.

Modern, yes of course it is — exciting, alive, and contagious. All across this land we have to get used to the idea that **change,** even a totally new language of vision and new explorations, is the contribution that artists must make to our universal curiosity about things of the spirit. Academic art and literal representation has little more to say in these serious and rapidly changing days. Oh yes, there is development and new life stirring.

It was inevitable that new forms of artistic expression should excite him. Lismer was always an innovator, had once been labelled a rebel, and was still the enemy of apathy. He often repeated the paradox that the most permanent thing in life was change. It might be for better or worse, but it was bound to occur. "Art is a barometer of change," he wrote on many occasions. He also believed that art foreshadowed these changes, even before they were apparent in the sciences or in social and economic affairs:

If the modern world expresses a poverty of soul, let the artist expose it. If it expresses an inherent force to which the people respond today, let the artist reveal it. (Let us) free the artist from the trammels of the past.

The modernist has been accused of superficiality; but that interpretation is superficial and thoroughly untrue. Art is "the child of its own times", and modernism is a misnomer. In the past, in relation to art, the ones who advertised the gospel story were modernists, and we are only now finding out that they used creative and unfolding methods, some of them quite in line with our modern ideas.

The modern artist, architect, or craftsman believes he is an interpreter of his age. (He) believes that art is not **there** and **then,** but **here** and **now.** (He) believes

140

that everything that exists today, the forms of trees and clouds, the hills and mountains here are just as beautiful as anything on the hillsides in Italy; that the light of our Canadian October is the equal of anything that prompted the Venetian painters. The same things move the people now in a rhythmic sense of beauty, but we have to interpret them differently, because we have a new scale of values.

It is curious that the academic mind, which would say "You can paint a peacock if you like," would say also that you must not paint a barnyard fowl, because the peacock has been the symbol of beauty right from the very earliest time, whereas the other is just a utility bird with a rather ugly exterior. You may paint a yacht in full sail, but you must not paint an oil tanker. One is a symbol of beauty and the other has no outline or content of beauty.

That is not the point of view of the present day worker in any of the arts. It is an absurd assumption, because the artist is not searching for perfection. I have never seen the perfect picture. I have heard it talked about in antique salesrooms, but I have never seen it. If you buy a thing and someone tells you that it is the most perfect expression of a master of the seventeenth century ... You swallow it because it happens to be connected with a work of art and art is adored. Just as we think that a door labelled "religion" leads into church, and only on Sundays and under compulsion, or one labelled "art" that leads one into an Art Gallery. These doors belong to the possessive individual who likes to carry around with him some little idea, part of a small bundle of sticks gathered years ago, scorning the fervour of youth and some of those mad-hat modern day colours and works in line and mass, and holding on to the old conventional and safe standards.

The modernist is not concerned with the imitation of life. Imitation has been called the sincerest form of flattery. Whistler said that imitation was a damned insult, and in trying to catch the fragrance of a flower and put it into pictorial form — that needs some doing — and the exact appearance of a butterfly's wing we lose contact with the thing the modernist is after, which is the significance rather than the outward form, the idea produced in the spectator or the one who is to create this thing, by a concentration on the designed order inside it all.... If the main channel has been adhered to it grows like a tree. We grow from the seed up to the fruit. But we think very often in terms of imagination. A concrete, definite photographic illusion — not so much an illusion as an actuality — stops the creative progression and appeases the curiosity right there.

Although there is no date on the lecture quoted above, it is likely that Lismer was referring to the contemporary art of the thirties. If it had been written in the fifties or sixties, he would have said much the same about the art of that period. How the artist reacts at any time is derived from his own experience, which he wishes to share. The public may accept his clarification of this experience or it may reject it. "But," said Lismer at this point, "it cannot dictate how it should be done."

What the real creative artist wants, and what he needs is wider sympathy and understanding of art and the artist in society. If we cannot provide a compelling motif for releasing the qualities and desires of the artist into useful service to society, then he will provide the only motif that he knows — himself. He will present a self disturbed, exalted, depressed, satirical, and powerfully abstract. It will express insecurity and challenge — but it will be art, and possibly great art. He will not deal with the forms and appearance of things seen, but with creating a pattern, or a design, of things felt — symbols, not appearances — designs, not likeness.

Too often (the artist's) abstractions are mere evidences of escape — realization that society today has no use for his creative exuberance and skill.... For the artist, then, there is no aim and purpose. All the beauty of creative form cannot be relegated to the decoration of life or to the museums. All the problems of life cannot be solved by machinery and politics. Watching the machinery of existence is not life. Spending our days in the engine room is not living.

According to Lismer the artist in the modern world, as in the past, has a social function. He must not live apart from what is happening in human affairs. On this theme, in 1933, my father wrote:

Art is a social function and production is life. Economic depression is a term used by big business. It cannot affect the spirit of art. If an artist has resentment against life it should be put into his work. We need a wholesome, national cleansing through another Daumier or Goya. There is enough in the pageant of life today to produce a host of rebellious artists. We need new symbolisms and dynamisms of forms — we need satire, and caricature, and great and powerful expressions of idealism in all the arts.

Dories, Cape Breton Island, 1948

Many of Lismer's topical and amusing cartoons were mild expressions of this national cleansing. In the mid-thirties, when there was much political unrest in the world, he produced a number of quick drawings that ranged from sly digs at the art critics to more pointed commentaries on international affairs. Since these drawings were topical and grew out of the moment, from this distance they have lost much of their impact. Although he admired the early political and social cartoonists, such as Hogarth and Daumier, and later Low, in England, he was not sure that there was a place for this idiom in Canada:

> I wonder if we Canadians could take it? In this sanitized, packeted, and pasteurized world of comfort and scientific protection, and the laws of libel, our great and near-great are more or less immune from such scurrilous thought as caricature.
>
> In England, the cartoonist Low and the journal *Punch* can give it, and the people can laugh at it, and the politicians ignore it — even like it — whether it was Chamberlain's umbrella or Winston Churchill's chins and cigar. But we have to subsist on imported Americanisms, in banal chatter and crude line, in comic strips and cartoons. We don't encourage Canadian artists to caricature our leading figures. What they do to our landscape is a matter of indifference.
>
> We have had few outstanding artists who have dared to venture into the field of caricature. Sometimes we could do with a little to recall to us our common human function of living and laughing together at our own foibles and peculiarities, not seen through American eyes.

The cartoons were not an important part of Lismer's work, but they provided a lot of fun for everyone. The quick sketches that he made, more or less to channel off his energy when he was idle for a short while, were effective comments on the passing scene. As portraits of people who caught his eye, the brief sketches were better likenesses than the laboured drawings that he made when a portrait was intended. He never regarded the latter as much good. The more time he spent on them the less satisfied he became. But a rapid scrawl with a few lines could catch both the spirit and the appearance of his target.

A . A DEW LAPPER

A BLOTSKY .

148

Composite Creatures, 1950

RINGNOSED WISKTAIL

My father drew everything and anything that appeared before him, or grew out of his imagination. Animals of all sorts were special favorites, charming and full of character. Not content with the species already in existence, he gave form to a whole menagerie of 'composite creatures'. One of these of which I was particularly fond was the *Ringnosed Wisktail*. In theory, these were drawn to amuse his three grand-daughters, but I know that many of them were done for his own entertainment.

Oriental Figures, 1955

Not only did Arthur Lismer have a vast amount of subject material, but he also liked to experiment with different styles. He made quick, simple line drawings emulating Matisse, or some abstract designs suggestive of Braque, whom he admired. He was also much intrigued with the art of China and Japan and used oriental brushes and black ink to follow the rhythms and flowing lines of Hokusai. These were not done with exhibitions or sales in mind, but for his own satisfaction — just to show himself that he could master other styles.

It was in the winter of 1960 that an event occurred that upset him, to some extent. An early-morning fire in the Children's Art Centre, near the Montreal Museum of Fine Arts, destroyed most of the interior of the building, and my father's office was badly damaged. He was reported to have lost most of his paintings and drawings that were stored there. To him, the real tragedy was the loss of valuable records of the work with children over many years. A newspaper account had him "surveying the loss of years of work and memories. The laugh was gone from his eyes. His tall, lean figure was bent with grief." But this did not sound like my father. I think he would have said: "Too bad! Now let's get the mess cleaned up and start again."

It was a shock, of course, as is any disaster that destroys personal property. But he was too busy to dwell on what was past and he was soon, once more, looking ahead. A few weeks later, in a letter to a friend in Toronto, he gave his own account of the incident:

> The holocaust set me off painting again, and of all subjects — Georgian Bay! Nostalgic, yes, but soul satisfying. (There must be psychological reasons!).... I am supposed to have lost 'all his life's work' in the fire. Actually, I had very few paintings left, except small canvases and 12 x 16 sketches and a lot of drawings. Counting up after the fire I figured I had lost about thirty 12 x 16 sketches and about six or eight 20 x 16 (the small canvases) and about one hundred drawings — no insurance. But also no loss to the world of art. Nearly all my library and teaching material — films — reproductions — records and notes — etc. And that's the story.

When they went to British Columbia for their summer vacation that year Lismer made up most of his losses. In a letter to me, written about two-thirds of the way through the holiday, he mentioned that he had done about thirty panels and thirty-five drawings.

My father was then 75, an age when many men had already retired, comfortably content to see the world slip past. But he felt that he still had pictures to paint and children to guide. Above all, there were still new experiences to share. He was not yet ready to step aside:

> No artist worth the name can afford to stand still. The world is too wonderful, too surprising in its new potentials for revelation of new vistas in the visible world, to say nothing of the invisible world of space. The new function of art has little to do with conventional appearance, or even beauty. We should, indeed, think it a strange world if our scientists stopped discovering, or if in industry, science, and technology there was nothing new. But everything is expanding, including the horizons of vision and art.

With such exciting promises ahead no wonder Arthur Lismer looked forward. He was not interested in reminiscing about events and attitudes that had served their purpose and had been replaced. The replacements, too, would change. New controversies would arise and new battles for the young artists. As long as this went on life would be bright and optimistic.

Painters and poets would continue to look to the future, pointing the way to a fuller life. Those who were adverse to change would cling to their familiar and comfortable ways. "But," declared my father, "it is stagnation for painters to look backwards."

Never Look Back, B.C. (undated)

List of Drawings

156